This book belongs to:

_____

_____

A TREASURY OF
NURSERY
RHYMES

Over 100 favourite rhymes

This edition published by Parragon Books Ltd in 2017

Parragon Books Ltd
Chartist House
15–17 Trim Street
Bath BA1 1HA, UK
www.parragon.com

ISBN 978-1-4748-5724-6

Printed in China

A TREASURY OF
NURSERY
RHYMES

Over 100 favourite rhymes

PaRragon

Bath · New York · Cologne · Melbourne · Delhi
Hong Kong · Shenzhen · Singapore

Contents

Classic Rhymes

Animal Rhymes

Counting Rhymes

Action Rhymes

Bedtime Rhymes

Classic Rhymes

Humpty Dumpty

Humpty Dumpty sat on a wall,
Humpty Dumpty had a

great f a l l.

All the king's horses, and all the king's men
Couldn't put Humpty together again!

The Grand Old Duke Of York

The grand old Duke of York,
He had ten thousand men.
He marched them up to the top of the hill
And he marched them down again.

When they were up, they were up.
And when they were down, they were down.
And when they were only halfway up,
They were neither up nor down.

Rain, Rain, Go Away

Rain, rain, go away,
Come again another day.
Little Johnny wants to play.

One Misty, Moisty Morning

One misty, moisty morning,
When cloudy was the weather,
There I met an old man
All clothed in leather.
He began to compliment
And I began to grin.
How do you do?
And how do you do?
And how do you do
AGAIN?

Oranges and Lemons

Oranges and lemons,
Say the bells of St Clement's.
You owe me five farthings,
Say the bells of St Martin's.
When will you pay me?
Say the bells of Old Bailey.
When I grow rich,
Say the bells of Shoreditch.

Boys and Girls Come Out to Play

Boys and girls, come out to play,
The moon doth shine as bright as day!
Leave your supper and leave your sleep,
And join your playfellows in the street.
Come with a whoop and come with a call,
Come with a good will or not at all.

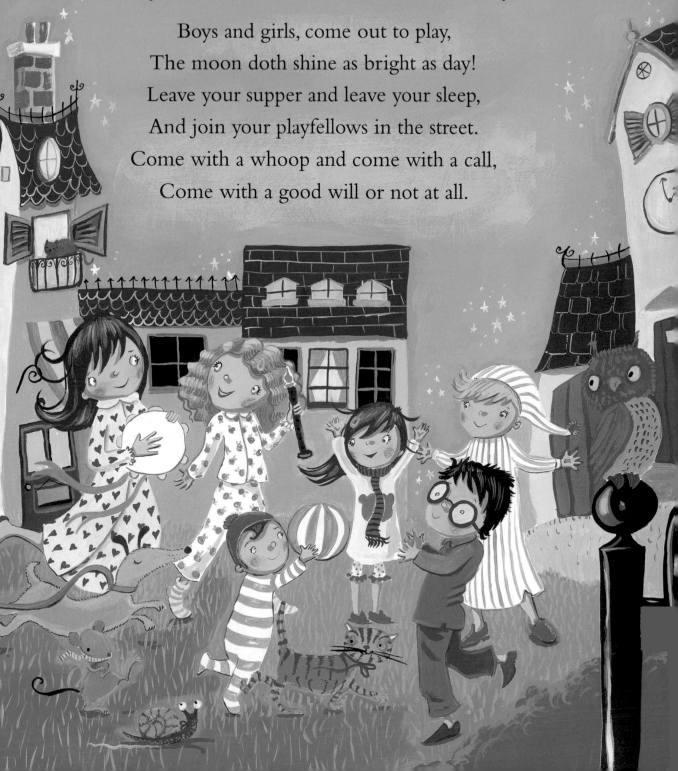

Old King Cole

Old King Cole was a merry old soul
And a merry old soul was he.
He called for his pipe in the middle of the night
And he called for his fiddlers three.

Every fiddler had a very fine fiddle
And a very fine fiddle had he.
Oh there's none so rare as can compare,
With King Cole and his fiddlers three.

See-Saw, Margery Daw

See-saw, Margery Daw,
Johnny shall have a new master.
He shall have but a penny a day,
Because he can't work any faster.

There Was An Old Woman

There was an old woman
Who lived in a shoe.
She had so many children
She didn't know what to do!

So she gave them some broth
Without any bread.
Then she whipped them all soundly
And sent them to bed.

What Are Little Boys Made Of?

What are little boys made of?

What are little boys made of?

Snips and snails,
And puppy-dogs' tails,

That's what little boys are made of.

What Are Little Girls Made Of?

What are little girls made of?

What are little girls made of?

Sugar and spice,
And all things nice,

That's what little girls are made of.

Simple Simon

Simple Simon met a pieman,
Going to the fair;
Said Simple Simon to the pieman,
"Let me taste your ware."

Said the pieman to Simple Simon,
"Show me first your penny."
Said Simple Simon to the pieman,
"Indeed I have not any."

Peter, Peter, Pumpkin Eater

Peter, Peter, pumpkin eater,
Had a wife and couldn't keep her;
He put her in a pumpkin shell
And there he kept her very well.

Monday's Child

Monday's child is fair of face,
Tuesday's child is full of grace,
Wednesday's child is full of woe,
Thursday's child has far to go,

Friday's child is loving and giving,
Saturday's child works hard for his living,
And the child that is born on the Sabbath day
Is bonny and blithe and good and gay.

Teddy Bears' Picnic

If you go out in the woods today
You're sure of a big surprise.
If you go out in the woods today
You'd better go in disguise!

For every bear that ever there was
Will gather there for certain, because
Today's the day the teddy bears have their picnic.

Peter Piper

Peter Piper picked a peck of pickled peppers;
A peck of pickled peppers Peter Piper picked;
If Peter Piper picked a peck of pickled peppers,
Where's the peck of pickled peppers Peter Piper picked?

This rhyme is a tongue-twister. Say it as quickly as you can.

Lavender's Blue

Lavender's blue, dilly, dilly,
Lavender's green,
When I am king, dilly, dilly,
You shall be queen.
Call up your men, dilly, dilly,
Set them to work,
Some with a rake, dilly, dilly,
Some with a fork.
Some to make hay, dilly, dilly,
Some to thresh corn,
While you and I, dilly, dilly,
Keep ourselves warm.

The Queen Of Hearts

The Queen of Hearts, she made some tarts
All on a summer's day.
The Knave of Hearts, he stole the tarts
And took them clean away.

The King of Hearts called for the tarts
And beat the Knave full sore.
The Knave of Hearts brought back the tarts
And vowed he'd steal no more.

The Big Ship Sails

The big ship sails on the ally-ally-oh,
The ally-ally-oh, the ally-ally-oh.
Oh, the big ship sails on the ally-ally-oh
On the last day of September.

The captain said it will never, never do,
Never, never do, never, never do.
The captain said it will never, never do
On the last day of September.

The big ship sank to the bottom of the sea,
The bottom of the sea, the bottom of the sea.
The big ship sank to the bottom of the sea
On the last day of September.

We all dip our heads in the deep blue sea,
The deep blue sea, the deep blue sea.
We all dip our heads in the deep blue sea
On the last day of September.

Pease-Pudding

Pease-pudding hot,
Pease-pudding cold,
Pease-pudding in the pot,
Nine days old.
Some like it hot,
Some like it cold,
Some like it in the pot,
Nine days old.

Jack Sprat

Jack Sprat could eat no fat,

His wife could eat no lean,

And so between the two of them

They licked the platter clean.

I Had A Little Nut Tree

I had a little nut tree,
Nothing would it bear,
But a silver nutmeg
And a golden pear.

The King of Spain's daughter
Came to visit me,
All for the sake
Of my little nut tree!

Robin Hood, Robin Hood

Robin Hood, Robin Hood,
Is in the mickle wood!
Little John, Little John,
He to the town is gone.

Hickory Dickory Dock

Hickory dickory dock,
The mouse ran up the clock.
The clock struck one,
The mouse ran down,
Hickory dickory dock.

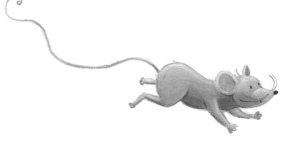

Tweedledum And Tweedledee

Tweedledum and Tweedledee
Agreed to have a battle,
For Tweedledum said Tweedledee
Had spoiled his nice new rattle.

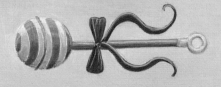

Just then flew down a monstrous crow,
As black as a tar-barrel,
Which frightened both the heroes so,
They quite forgot their quarrel.

43

Little Miss Muffet

Little Miss Muffet
Sat on a tuffet,
Eating her curds and whey.

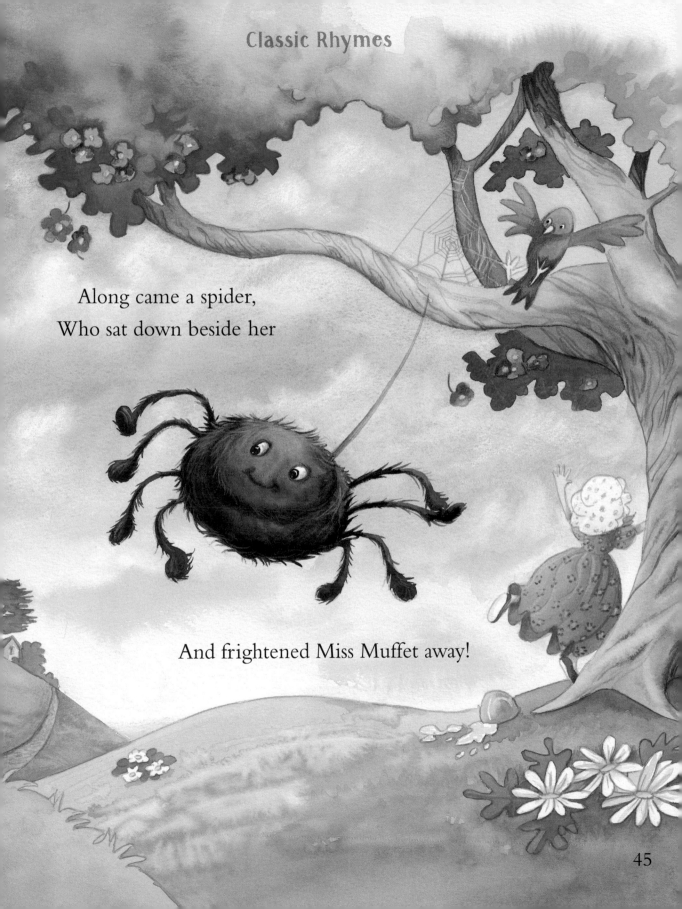

Along came a spider,
Who sat down beside her

And frightened Miss Muffet away!

Doctor Foster

Doctor Foster

Went to Gloucester

In a shower of rain.

He stepped in a puddle,

Right up to his middle,

And never went there again!

Bobby Shaftoe

Bobby Shaftoe's gone to sea,
Silver buckles at his knee;
He'll come back and marry me,
Bonny Bobby Shaftoe!

The House that Jack Built

This is the house that Jack built.

This is the man all tattered and torn,

That kissed the maiden all forlorn,

That milked the cow with the crumpled horn,

That tossed the dog,

That worried the cat,

That killed the rat,

That ate the malt

That lay in the house that Jack built.

Animal Rhymes

Little Bo-Peep

Little Bo-Peep has lost her sheep
And doesn't know where to find them.

Leave them alone
And they'll come home,
Wagging their tails behind them.

Baa, Baa, Black Sheep

Baa, baa, black sheep,
Have you any wool?

Yes sir, yes sir,
Three bags full.

One for the master…

And one for the dame…

And one for the little boy
Who lives down the lane.

The Little White Duck

There's a little white duck, "Quack!"
Sitting in the water.
A little white duck, "Quack!"
Doing what he oughter.
He took a bite of a lily pad,
Flapped his wings and he said,
"I'm glad I'm a little white duck
Sitting in the water.
Quack, quack, quack!"

Haymaking

The maids in the meadow
Are making the hay,
The ducks in the river
Are swimming away.

Hey Diddle Diddle

Hey diddle diddle, the cat and the fiddle,

The cow jumped over the moon.

The little dog laughed to see such fun

And the dish ran away with the spoon!

The Owl And The Pussy Cat

The Owl and the Pussy Cat went to sea
In a beautiful pea-green boat,
They took some honey, and plenty of money,
Wrapped up in a five pound note.

The Owl looked up to the stars above,
And sang to a small guitar,
"Oh lovely Pussy! Oh Pussy, my love,
What a beautiful Pussy you are, you are, you are,
What a beautiful Pussy you are."

Pussy said to the Owl, "You elegant fowl,
How charmingly sweet you sing.
Oh let us be married, too long we have tarried.
But what shall we do for a ring?"

Animal Rhymes

They sailed away, for a year and a day,
To the land where the Bong-tree grows,
And there in a wood a Piggy-wig stood
With a ring at the end of his nose, his nose, his nose,
With a ring at the end of his nose.

Ladybird, Ladybird

Ladybird, ladybird, fly away home;
Your house is on fire, your children all gone,
All except one, and that's little Ann,
And she hid under the baking pan.

Goosey, Goosey, Gander

Goosey, goosey, gander,
Whither do you wander?
Upstairs and downstairs
And in my lady's chamber.

There I met an old man
Who would not say his prayers,
So I took him by the left leg,
And threw him down the stairs.

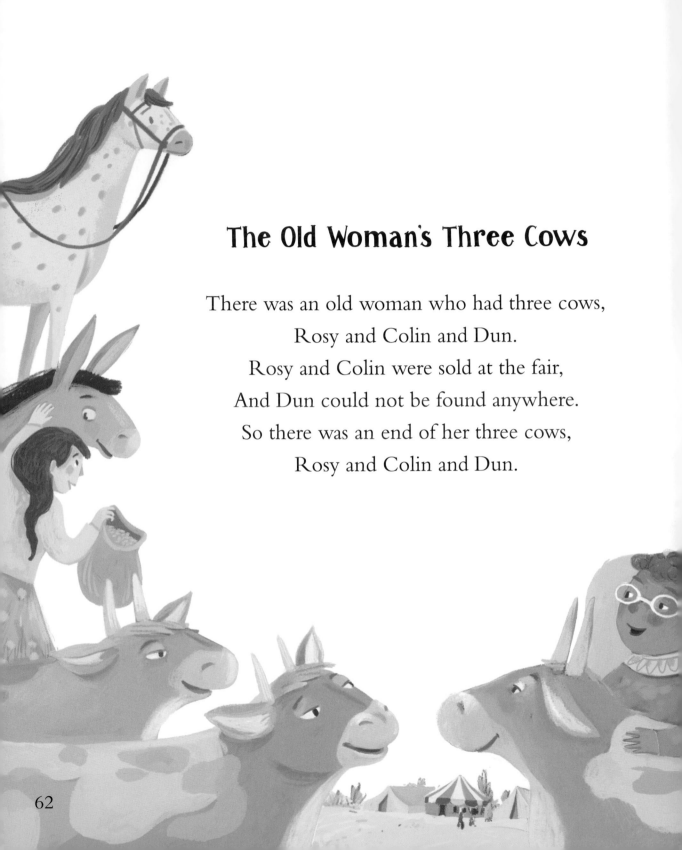

The Old Woman's Three Cows

There was an old woman who had three cows,
Rosy and Colin and Dun.
Rosy and Colin were sold at the fair,
And Dun could not be found anywhere.
So there was an end of her three cows,
Rosy and Colin and Dun.

If Pigs Could Fly

If pigs could fly
High in the sky,
Where do you think they'd go?
Would they follow a plane
To France or Spain,
Or drift where the wind blows?

Mary Had A Little Lamb

Mary had a little lamb,
Its fleece was white as snow,
And everywhere that Mary went

The lamb was sure to go.

Animal Rhymes

It followed her to school one day,
Which was against the rule.
It made the children laugh and play
To see a lamb at school.

Little Boy Blue

Little Boy Blue,
Come blow your horn.
The sheep's in the meadow,
The cow's in the corn.
Where is the boy who looks after the sheep?
He's under a haycock, fast asleep.
Will you wake him?
No, not I, for if I do, he's sure to cry.

Cock-a-Doodle-Doo!

Cock-a-doodle-doo!
My dame has lost her shoe!
My master's lost his fiddling stick,
And doesn't know what to do.

Old MacDonald Had a Farm

Old MacDonald had a farm,
Ee-i-ee-i-o!
And on that farm he had a cow,
Ee-i-ee-i-o!
With a moo-moo here,
And a moo-moo there,
Here a moo, there a moo,
Everywhere a moo-moo,
Old MacDonald had a farm,
Ee-i-ee-i-o!

Tom, Tom, the Piper's Son

Tom, Tom, the piper's son,
Stole a pig and away he ran.
The pig was eat, and Tom was beat,
And Tom went roaring down the street.

I Had A Little Hen

I had a little hen,
The prettiest ever seen,
She washed up the dishes,
And kept the house clean.

She went to the mill
To fetch me some flour,
And always got home
In less than an hour.

She baked me my bread,
She brewed me my ale,
She sat by the fire
And told a fine tale!

Sing A Song Of Sixpence

Sing a song of sixpence
A pocket full of rye.
Four and twenty blackbirds
Baked in a pie.
When the pie was opened
The birds began to sing.
Now wasn't that a dainty dish
To set before the king?

Animal Rhymes

The king was in his counting house
Counting out his money.
The queen was in the parlour
Eating bread and honey.
The maid was in the garden
Hanging out the clothes,
When down came a blackbird
And pecked off
her nose!

First In A Carriage

First in a carriage,
Second in a gig,
Third on a donkey,
And fourth on a pig.

Slowly, Slowly

Slowly, slowly, very slowly
Creeps the garden snail.
Slowly, slowly, very slowly
Up the garden rail.

Quickly, quickly, very quickly
Runs the little mouse.
Quickly, quickly, very quickly
Round about the house.

Three Blind Mice

Three blind mice, three blind mice,
See how they run, see how they run!
They all ran after the farmer's wife,
Who cut off their tails with a carving knife,
Did you ever see such a thing in your life
As three blind mice?

Counting Rhymes

Two Little Dickie Birds

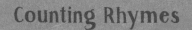

Two little dickie birds sitting on a wall,
One named Peter, one named Paul.

Counting Rhymes

Fly away Peter, fly away Paul.

Come back Peter, come back Paul.

One Potato, Two Potato

One potato,

Two potato,

Three potato,

Four.

Five potato,

Counting Rhymes

Six potato,

Seven potato,

Counting Rhymes

More!

Five Little Ducks

Five little ducks went swimming one day,
Over the hills and far away.
Mother Duck said, "Quack, quack, quack, quack,"
But only four little ducks came back.
*(Repeat the rhyme, counting down from four little ducks
to one little duck…)*
One little duck went swimming one day,
Over the hills and far away.
Mother Duck said, "Quack, quack, quack, quack,"
But none of the five little ducks came back.

Mother Duck went swimming one day,
Over the hills and far away.
Mother Duck said, "Quack, quack, quack, quack,"
And five little ducks came swimming back.

Five Fat Peas

Five fat peas in a pea-pod pressed,
One grew, two grew, so did all the rest.

They grew, and grew,
And did not stop,
Until one day,

the pod went

POP!

One Man Went To Mow

One man went to mow,
Went to mow a meadow,
One man, and his dog,
Went to mow a meadow.
Two men went to mow,
Went to mow a meadow,
Two men, one man, and his dog,
Went to mow a meadow.

Three men went to mow,
Went to mow a meadow,
Three men, two men,
one man, and his dog,
Went to mow a meadow.
Four men went to mow,
Went to mow a meadow,
Four men, three men, two men,
one man, and his dog,
Went to mow a meadow.

*(You can keep adding verses as far
as you can count.)*

One, Two, Buckle My Shoe

One, two, buckle my shoe,

Three, four, knock at the door,

Five, six, pick up sticks,

Seven, eight, lay them straight,

Nine, ten, a big fat hen,

Eleven, twelve, dig and delve,

Thirteen, fourteen, maids a-courting,

Fifteen, sixteen,
maids in the kitchen,

Seventeen,
eighteen,
maids in waiting,

Nineteen, twenty,
my plate's empty!

One, Two, Three, Four, Five

One, two, three, four, five,

Once I caught a fish alive.

Six, seven, eight, nine, ten,

Then I let it go again.

Counting Rhymes

Why did you let it go?
Because it bit my finger so.
Which finger did it bite?
This little finger on the right.

Five Little Monkeys

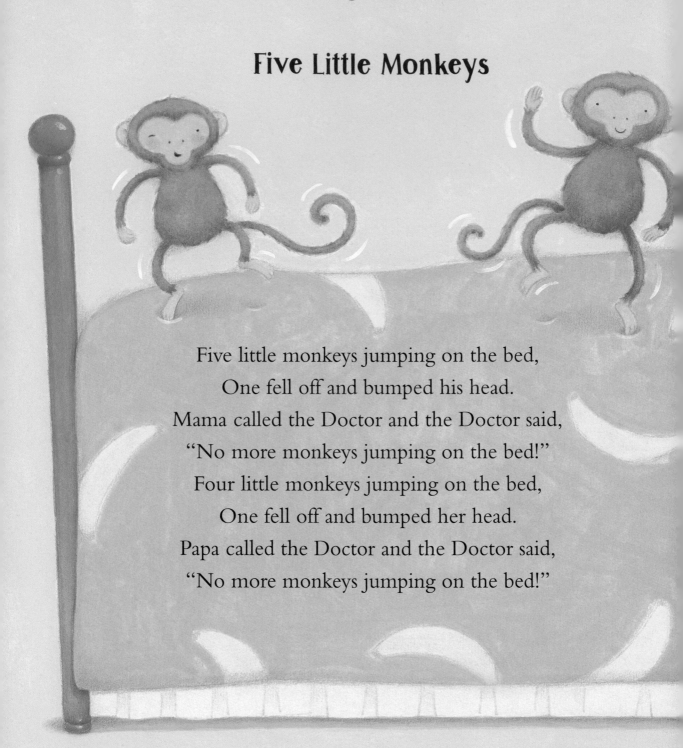

Five little monkeys jumping on the bed,
One fell off and bumped his head.
Mama called the Doctor and the Doctor said,
"No more monkeys jumping on the bed!"
Four little monkeys jumping on the bed,
One fell off and bumped her head.
Papa called the Doctor and the Doctor said,
"No more monkeys jumping on the bed!"

*(Repeat the rhyme, counting down from three
little monkeys to one little monkey…)*

One little monkey jumping on the bed,
He fell off and bumped his head.
Mama called the Doctor and the Doctor said,
"Put those monkeys straight to bed!"

One For Sorrow

One for sorrow,

Two for joy,

Counting Rhymes

Three for a girl,

Four for a boy,

99

Five for silver,

Six for gold,

Seven for a secret, never to be told.

This Old Man

This old man, he played one,
He played knick-knack on my drum.

(Chorus)

With a knick-knack, paddy whack,
Give a dog a bone,
This old man came rolling home.

This old man, he played two,
He played knick-knack on my shoe.

(Chorus)

This old man, he played three,
He played knick-knack on my knee.

(Chorus)

This old man, he played four,
He played knick-knack on my door.

(Chorus)

Counting Rhymes

This old man, he played five,
He played knick-knack on my hive.

(Chorus)

This old man, he played six,
He played knick-knack on my sticks.

(Chorus)

This old man, he played seven,
He played knick-knack up to heaven.

(Chorus)

Counting Rhymes

This old man, he played eight,
He played knick-knack on my gate.

(Chorus)

This old man, he played nine,
He played knick-knack on my spine.

(Chorus)

This old man, he played ten,
He played knick-knack once again.

(Chorus)

Ten Green Bottles

Ten green bottles sitting on the wall,
Ten green bottles sitting on the wall,
And if one green bottle should accidentally fall,
There'd be nine green bottles sitting on the wall.

Nine green bottles sitting on the wall,
Nine green bottles sitting on the wall,
And if one green bottle should accidentally fall,
There'd be eight green bottles sitting on the wall.

Eight green bottles sitting on the wall,

Eight green bottles sitting on the wall,

And if one green bottle should accidentally fall,

There'd be seven green bottles sitting on the wall.

Seven green bottles sitting on the wall,

Seven green bottles sitting on the wall,

And if one green bottle should accidentally fall,

There'd be six green bottles sitting on the wall.

(You can keep adding verses until there are no more bottles!)

Rub-A-Dub-Dub

Rub-a-dub-dub,
Three men in a tub,
And how do you think they got there?

The butcher, the baker
The candlestick maker,

They all jumped out of a rotten potato,
It was enough to make a man stare.

Five Fat Sausages

Five fat sausages sizzling in the pan,
All of a sudden one went

BANG!

Four fat sausages sizzling in the pan,
All of a sudden one went

BANG!

Three fat sausages sizzling in the pan,
All of a sudden one went

BANG!

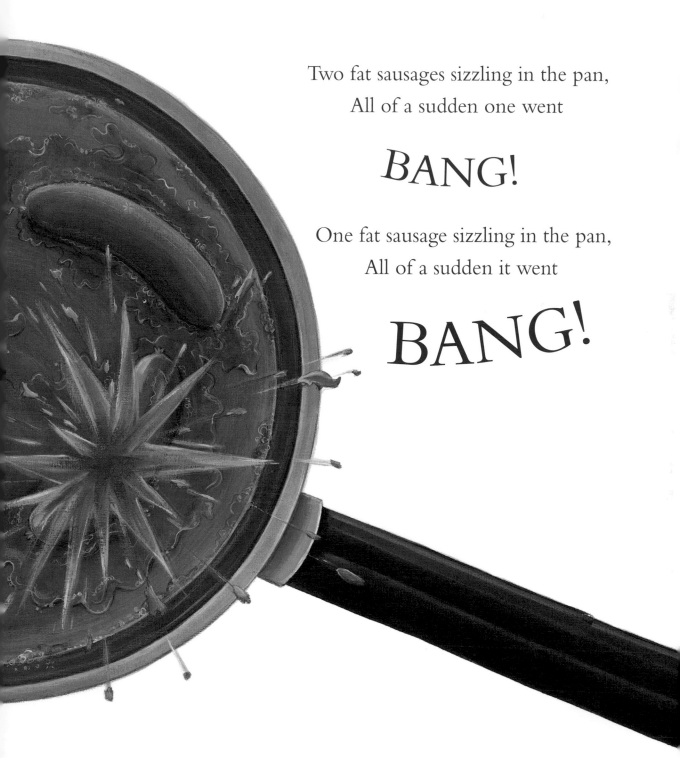

Two fat sausages sizzling in the pan,
All of a sudden one went

BANG!

One fat sausage sizzling in the pan,
All of a sudden it went

BANG!

Five Currant Buns

Five currant buns in the baker's shop,
Big and round with a cherry on the top.
Along came *(insert name)* with a penny one day,
Bought a currant bun and took it away.
Four currant buns in the baker's shop,
Big and round with a cherry on the top.
Along came *(insert name)* with a penny one day,
Bought a currant bun and took it away.
(Repeat the rhyme, counting down from
three currant buns to no currant buns…)

Counting Rhymes

No currant buns in the baker's shop,
Nothing big and round with a cherry on the top.
Along came *(insert name)* with a penny one day,
"Sorry," said the baker,
"No more currant buns today."

Five Little Speckled Frogs

Five little speckled frogs,
Sat on a speckled log,
Eating the most delicious bugs,
Yum, yum!
One jumped into the pool,
Where it was nice and cool.
Now there are four green speckled frogs,
Glub, glub!
*(Repeat the rhyme, counting down from five little speckled
frogs to one little speckled frog…)*

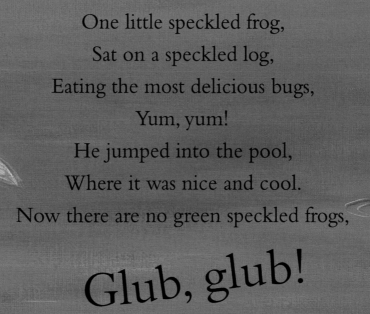

One little speckled frog,
Sat on a speckled log,
Eating the most delicious bugs,
Yum, yum!
He jumped into the pool,
Where it was nice and cool.
Now there are no green speckled frogs,

Glub, glub!

Ten Little Teddies

Ten little teddies, standing in a line,
One of them went fishing, so then there were nine.
Nine little teddies, marching through a gate,
One stopped to tie his shoe, so then there were eight.

Eight little teddies, floating up in heaven,
One fell down and broke his crown, so then there were seven.
Seven little teddies, doing magic tricks,
One made himself disappear, so then there were six.

Six little teddies, about to take a dive,
One of them was scared of heights, so then there were five.
Five little teddies, running on the shore,
One went surfing in the waves, so then there were four.

Counting Rhymes

Four little teddies, eating cakes for tea,
One of them was feeling sick, so then there were three.
Three little teddies, heading for the zoo,
One thought he'd take the bus, so then there were two.

Two little teddies, playing in the sun,
One of them got sunburned, so then there was one.
One little teddy, who's had lots of fun,
It's time for him to go to sleep, so now there are none.

Ten In The Bed

There were ten in the bed and the little one said,
"Roll over, roll over."
So they all rolled over and one fell out.

There were nine in the bed and the little one said,
"Roll over, roll over."
So they all rolled over and one fell out.

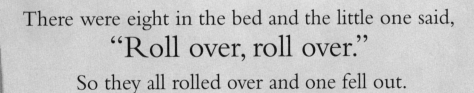

There were eight in the bed and the little one said,
"Roll over, roll over."
So they all rolled over and one fell out.

There were seven in the bed and the little one said,
"Roll over, roll over."
So they all rolled over and one fell out.

Counting Rhymes

There were six in the bed and the little one said,
"Roll over, roll over."
So they all rolled over and one fell out.

*(Repeat the rhyme, counting down from five in the bed
to one in the bed…)*

There was one in the bed and the little one said,

"Goodnight!"

Hot Cross Buns!

Hot cross buns!
Hot cross buns!
One a penny, two a penny,
Hot cross buns!
If you have no daughters,
Give them to your sons.
One a penny, two a penny,
Hot cross buns!

Action Rhymes

Row, Row, Row Your Boat

(Mime a rowing action throughout as the rhyme suggests.)

Row, row, row your boat
Gently down the stream.

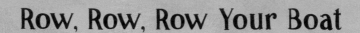

Merrily, merrily, merrily, merrily,

Life is but a dream.

I'm A Little Teapot

I'm a little teapot, short and stout,

Here's my handle,

(Place one hand on your hip.)

here's my spout.

(Other arm out with elbow and wrist bent.)

When I get my steam up hear me shout,

Tip me up and
pour me out.

(Lean over as if you're pouring out the tea.)

Catch It If You Can

Mix a pancake,
Beat a pancake,
Put it in a pan.
Cook a pancake,
Toss a pancake,
Catch it if you can!

Georgie Porgie

Georgie Porgie, pudding and pie,
Kissed the girls, and made them cry.
When the boys came out to play,
Georgie Porgie ran away.

Round And Round The Garden

Round and round the garden
Like a teddy bear.
*(Draw a circle on the palm of your baby's hand
with your finger.)*

One step,
Two steps,
(Walk your fingers up your baby's arm.)
Tickle you under there!
(Tickle baby under the arm.)

131

This Little Piggy

(Pretend each of the child's toes is a little piggy.
Begin with the biggest toe and finish by tickling under the child's foot.)

This little piggy went to market,

This little piggy stayed at home,

This little piggy
had roast beef,

This little piggy
had none,

And this little piggy cried,
  "Wee, wee, wee!"
  all the way home.

If You're Happy and You Know It

If you're happy and you know it,
Clap your hands.
If you're happy and you know it,
Clap your hands.
If you're happy and you know it,
And you really want to show it,
If you're happy and you know it,
Clap your hands.

Action Rhymes

If you're happy and you know it,
Nod your head, etc.

If you're happy and you know it,
Stamp your feet, etc.

If you're happy and you know it,
Say "We are!", etc.

If you're happy and you know it,
Do all four!

I Hear Thunder

I hear thunder, I hear thunder,
Hark, don't you? Hark, don't you?
Pitter-patter raindrops,
Pitter-patter raindrops,

I'm wet through,
So are you.

Pat-A-Cake, Pat-A-Cake

Pat-a-cake, pat-a-cake, baker's man,

Bake me a cake as fast as you can.

(Clap in rhythm.)

Pat it and prick it and mark it with B,

(Pat and 'prick' palm,

then trace the letter B on palm.)

And put it in the oven for Baby and me!

(Action of putting cake in oven.)

Incy Wincy Spider

Incy Wincy Spider
Climbing up the spout.
Down came the rain
And washed the spider out.

Out came the sun
And dried up all the rain.
Incy Wincy Spider
Climbed up the spout again.

The Wheels On The Bus

The wheels on the bus go
Round and round!

Round and round!
Round and round!

The wheels on the bus go

round...

and...round!.
All day long.
(Move hands in a circular motion.)

The wipers on the bus go
Swish, swish, swish!
Swish, swish, swish!
Swish, swish, swish!
The wipers on the bus go
Swish, swish, swish!

All day long.

(Wiggle both index fingers.)

The horn on the bus goes
Beep, beep, beep!
Beep, beep, beep!
Beep, beep, beep!
The horn on the bus goes
Beep, beep, beep!

The people on the bus go
Chat, chat, chat!
Chat, chat, chat!
Chat, chat, chat!
The people on the bus go
Chat, chat, chat!

All day long.

All day long.

(Pretend to press a horn.)

(Hold your thumb and fingers out straight to make a beak shape and open and close it.)

Here Is The Church

Here is the church,
(Interlace fingers.)

Here is the steeple,
*(Put up both pointing fingers
to make a steeple.)*

146

Look inside…
(*Turn both hands over.*)

And see all the people!
(*Wiggle your fingers.*)

This Is The Way

This is the way we wash our hands,
Wash our hands, wash our hands.
This is the way we wash our hands
So early in the morning.

*(Repeat the rhyme four more times,
using these different actions.)*

This is the way we wash our face.

This is the way we brush our teeth.

This is the way we comb our hair.

This is the way we wave goodbye.

149

Teddy Bear, Teddy Bear

Teddy bear, teddy bear,
Touch the ground.
Teddy bear, teddy bear,
Turn around.
Teddy bear, teddy bear,
Walk upstairs.
Teddy bear, teddy bear,
Say your prayers.

Anna Maria

Anna Maria she sat on the fire;
The fire was too hot, she sat on the pot;
The pot was too round, she sat on the ground;
The ground was too flat, she sat on the cat;
The cat ran away with Maria on her back.

Here We Go Round The Mulberry Bush

Here we go round the mulberry bush,
The mulberry bush, the mulberry bush.
Here we go round the mulberry bush,
On a cold and frosty morning.

(Repeat the
rhyme three more times,
using these different actions.)

This is the way we
clean the house.

This is the way we
wash our clothes.

This is the way we
sweep the floor.

Ring-A-Ring O' Roses

Ring-a-ring o' roses,
A pocket full of posies.

A-tishoo! A-tishoo!
We all fall down.

Ride A Cock-Horse

Ride a cock-horse to Banbury Cross
To see a fine lady upon a white horse.
With rings on her fingers and bells on her toes,
She shall have music wherever she goes.

The Little Bird

This little bird flaps its wings,
Flaps its wings, flaps its wings,
This little bird flaps its wings,
And flies away in the morning!

Once I Saw a Little Bird

Once I saw a little bird
Come hop, hop, hop;
So I cried, "Little bird,
Will you stop, stop, stop?"
I was going to the window,
To say, "How do you do?"
But he shook his little tail,
And far away he flew.

Sippity Sup, Sippity Sup

Sippity sup, sippity sup,
Bread and milk from a china cup.
Bread and milk from a bright silver spoon
Made of a piece of the bright silver moon.

Sippity sup, sippity sup,
Sippity,
sippity sup.

160

Bedtime Rhymes

Come To Bed, Says Sleepy-Head

"Come to bed," says Sleepy-head,

"Tarry a while," says Slow,

"Put on the pot," says Greedy-guts,

"Let's sup before we go."

Bed In Summer

In winter I get up at night,

And dress by yellow candle-light.

In summer, quite the other way,

I have to go to bed by day.

I have to go to bed and see

The birds still hopping on the tree,

Or hear the grown-up people's feet

Still going past me in the street.

Bedtime Rhymes

And does it not seem hard to you,
When all the sky is clear and blue,
And I should like so much to play,
To have to go to bed by day?

Brahms' Lullaby

Lullaby, and good night,
With rosy bed light,
With lilies overspread,
Is my baby's sweet bed.

Bedtime Rhymes

Lay you down now, and rest,
May your slumber be blessed!
Lay you down now, and rest,
May your slumber be blessed!

Lullaby, and good night,
You're your mother's delight,
Shining angels beside
My darling abide.

Soft and warm is your bed,
Close your eyes and rest your head.
Soft and warm is your bed,
Close your eyes and rest your head.

Twinkle, Twinkle, Little Star

Twinkle, twinkle, little star,
How I wonder what you are!
Up above the world so high,
Like a diamond in the sky.
When the blazing sun is gone,
When he nothing shines upon,
Then you show your little light,
Twinkle, twinkle all the night.

Then the traveller in the dark,

Thanks you for your tiny spark,

He could not see which way to go,

If you did not twinkle so.

In the dark blue sky you keep,

And often through my curtains peep,

For you never shut your eye,

Till the sun is in the sky.

As your bright and tiny spark,

Lights the traveller in the dark.

Though I know not what you are,

Twinkle, twinkle, little star.

Go To Bed Late

Go to bed late,
Stay very small.

Go to bed early,
Grow very tall.

Go To Bed, Tom

Go to bed, Tom,
Go to bed, Tom,
Tired or not, Tom,
Go to bed, Tom.

Now The Day Is Over

Now the day is over,
Night is drawing nigh,
Shadows of the evening
Steal across the sky.

Now the darkness gathers,
Stars begins to peep,
Birds and beasts and flowers
Soon will be asleep.

Golden Slumbers

Golden slumbers kiss your eyes,
Smiles await you when you rise.
Sleep, pretty baby, do not cry,

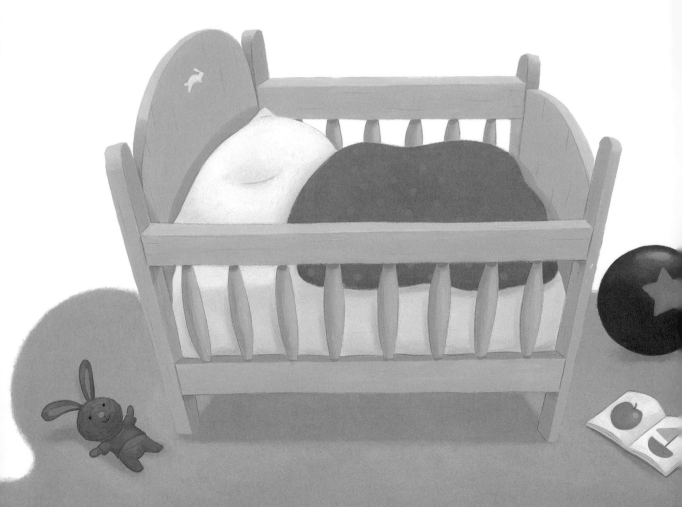

And I will sing
a lullaby.

Wee Willie Winkie

Wee Willie Winkie
Runs through the town,
Upstairs and downstairs
In his nightgown.
Rapping at the window,
Crying through the lock,
"Are the children all in bed?
It's past eight o'clock."

How Many Miles To Babylon?

How many miles to Babylon?
Three score and ten.
Can I get there by candle-light?
Yes, and back again.

BABYLON

If your heels are nimble and light,
You may get there by candle-light.

Hush, Little Baby

Hush, little baby, don't say a word,
Papa's gonna buy you a mocking bird.

If that mocking bird don't sing,
Papa's gonna buy you a diamond ring.

If that diamond ring turns to brass,
Papa's gonna buy you a looking-glass.

If that looking-glass gets broke,
Papa's gonna buy you a billy goat.

Bedtime Rhymes

If that billy goat don't pull,
Papa's gonna buy you a cart and mule.

If that cart and mule turn over,
Papa's gonna buy you a dog named Rover.

If that dog named Rover won't bark,
Papa's gonna buy you a horse and cart.

If that horse and cart fall down,
You'll still be the sweetest little baby in town.

Rock-A-Bye, Baby

Rock-a-bye, baby, on the tree top,
When the wind blows, the cradle will rock.

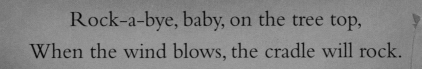

When the bough breaks,
The cradle will fall,

Down will come baby, cradle and all.

Sleep, Baby, Sleep

Sleep, baby, sleep,
Your father keeps the sheep;
Your mother shakes the dreamland tree
And from it fall sweet dreams for thee;
Sleep, baby, sleep.

Sleep, baby, sleep,
The large stars are the sheep;
The little stars are the lambs, I guess,
And the gentle moon is the shepherdess;
Sleep, baby, sleep.

Sleep, baby, sleep,
Your father keeps the sheep;
Your mother guards the lambs this night,
And keeps them safe till morning light;
Sleep, baby, sleep.

Red Sky at Night

Red sky at night, shepherd's delight.
Red sky in the morning, shepherd's warning.

185

I See the Moon

I see the moon and the moon sees me.
God bless the moon and God bless me.

Dance to Your Daddy

Dance to your daddy,
My little babby;
Dance to your daddy,
My little lamb.

You shall have a fishy,
In a little dishy;
You shall have a fishy
When the boat comes in.

Star Light, Star Bright

Star light,
Star bright,
First star
I see tonight,

I wish I may,
I wish I might,
Have the wish
I wish tonight.

Index Of First Lines